FACET BOOKS

HISTORICAL SERIES

F A C E T **fb** B O O K S

HISTORICAL SERIES — 6

(American Church)

Richard C. Wolf, Editor

The Formation of the American Catholic Minority 1820-1860

by THOMAS T. McAVOY

FORTRESS PRESS   PHILADELPHIA

This study was first published as "The Formation of the Catholic Minority in the United States 1820-1860" in *The Review of Politics* (South Bend, Indiana), X (January, 1948), 13-34, and is republished by arrangement with the publisher.

Published by Fortress Press, 1967

Library of Congress Catalog Card Number 67–22985

4082E67   Printed in U.S.A.   1-3042

Introduction

THE application of the spirit and policy of *aggiorna-mento* to the Roman Catholic Church, inaugurated by Pope John XXIII (1958-1963) and advanced by the Second Vatican Council, has had some results which were not only unpremeditated but, in all probability, unanticipated.

Among the more significant of these results have been: (1) an increased willingness on the part of American non-Roman Catholics[1] to accept Roman Catholics in a way never before experienced in American history; (2) the quest for an understanding of Roman Catholicism by non-Roman Catholics as the basis for an expanded and more amicable relationship; (3) the amelioration of relationships between non-Roman Catholics and Roman Catholics with a consequent decline in prejudice and polemics on both sides.

That these results have worked a change for the better seems scarcely debatable. There was a time when the attitude of many American non-Roman Catholics toward the papal church seemed to be motivated by uninformed prejudice; a time when such research as was made by non-

[1] "Non-Roman Catholic" is used throughout this introduction in place of the conventional but confusing "Protestant" because a goodly segment of the non-Roman Catholics is not historically, and in some instances does not claim to be, Protestant.

61358

Roman Catholics into the life, beliefs, history, attitudes and programs of the Roman Catholic Church was very often motivated by polemic intent.[2] Little attempt was made to deal objectively with the Roman Catholic Church, or to understand or empathize with that body. Indeed, the objectivity displayed by Jaroslav Pelikan in his book *The Riddle of Roman Catholicism*,[3] published in 1959, was hailed with pleased surprise by Roman Catholics, and, in some parts, repudiated by non-Roman Catholics.

Now a new day seems to have dawned. Roman Catholics and non-Roman Catholics are meeting together in the quest for mutual understanding and acceptance. Approaches to understanding are being made with candor and sincerity by both parties to the conversations. The stigma of being a minority group which is both feared and reprobated as being invidious to, if not subversive of, "The American Way of Life" is being expunged from the public estimate of Roman Catholics. Furthermore, Roman Catholics are increasingly assuming their rightfully representative place in American society, politics, education, and business.

Not all of this is the result of the labors of Pope John XXIII and Vatican II. To a fairly large degree the changes in attitudes and relationships have been due to the fact that Roman Catholic immigrants, who originally had stood aloof and consequently incurred the suspicion of the more militant exponents of "The American Way," have increasingly adapted to and been assimilated into the Protestant-oriented American culture.

In contradistinction to the remarkable degree of acclimatization achieved by the early colonial English Roman Catholics, the Irish and German immigrants of the middle and

[2] Paul Blanshard, *American Freedom and Catholic Power* (Boston: The Beacon Press, 1949) exemplifies this approach.

[3] Jaroslav Pelikan, *The Riddle of Roman Catholicism* (New York-Nashville: Abingdon Press, 1959).

latter nineteenth century tended either to isolate themselves from or resist outright the inroads of cultural acclimatization. Some Irish Roman Catholic leaders, most notably Archbishop John Hughes of New York,[4] actually feared acclimatization as a threat to the purity of the Roman Catholic faith. The result was that these large blocs of immigrant Roman Catholics were considered "alien invaders" whose adjustment to the American environment seemed impeded by their ecclesiastical affiliation. Arriving in the late nineteenth century, Italian and southern European Roman Catholics repeated the pattern and reenforced the reluctance of a large portion of the Roman Church to enter unreservedly into American patterns and ways of living. However, after the flow of immigration slowed in the years following 1921[5] the process of acclimatization picked up tempo in nearly equal proportion. Thus, by 1960, the degree of acculturization of at least the Roman Catholics of Irish origin was such that it was possible for one of their number, John Fitzgerald Kennedy, to be elected President of the United States.

In his essay Father Thomas T. McAvoy does more than make it unmistakably clear that Roman Catholics are not and never have been the monolithic cultural, political, and religious bloc that they have frequently been feared to be. He lays bare the internal tensions and conflicts among Roman Catholics which were created by the successive waves of immigration bringing English, French, Irish, and German Roman Catholics to American shores up to 1860.

Thomas T. McAvoy is a graduate of Notre Dame University. He received a Master of Arts degree from his alma mater and a Ph.D. from Columbia University. At the time

---

[4] McAvoy asserts, "Culturally the policy of Hughes set back the progress of the Irish immigrant at least a generation. . . ." See p. 20.

[5] After 1921 the flow of immigration was regulated by the nationality quota system which was applied in that year.

of his ordination to the priesthood in 1929 his original plan was to go into the field of American Philosophy. That plan was changed, however, when he was asked to take charge of Notre Dame University's vast but neglected collection of materials related to American Catholic history. Father McAvoy describes the change that this new vocational situation effected. "While my interests were now reversed and my major interest was American Catholic History, the problem of the relationship between the Catholic tradition and the general American culture remained intact. Eventually, I began to call the Catholic American tradition the history of the Catholic minority. The idea of Minority has not been universally welcomed, but I had intended no political or divisive purpose. I merely wanted to clarify the relationship between the ideals of the Catholic people in this country and those of their neighbors."[6]

For nearly forty years Father McAvoy has worked assiduously and productively at his task. He has produced numerous monographs dealing with the relationship of American Roman Catholicism with its environment and religious neighbors. Three major books have treated the same general area, *The Catholic Church in Indiana* (New York: Columbia University Press, 1940), *The Great Crisis in American Catholic History, 1895-1900* (Chicago: Henry Regnery Company, 1957), and *The Americanist Heresy in Roman Catholicism, 1895-1900* (Notre Dame: The University of Notre Dame Press, 1963). He has in manuscript form a history of the Catholic Church in the United States which he plans to revise for publication, utilizing his "Catholic minority" theme as the basic structure of the revision.

RICHARD C. WOLF

The Divinity School, Vanderbilt University
Nashville, Tennessee, June, 1967

[6] Personal letter from Thomas T. McAvoy, C.S.C., to Richard C. Wolf, October 31, 1966.

THE FORMATION OF
THE AMERICAN CATHOLIC MINORITY
1820-1860

No minority group in the United States is probably as formless and yet at the same time as rigid as the American membership of the Roman Catholic Church. The rigidity of the Catholic organization arises from the fact that there has never been a real heresy during the three centuries and more of Catholic life within the boundaries of the present United States. Even the so-called heresy of Americanism[1] existed more in the minds of European theologians than in the Catholics of the New World. There have been diver-

---

[1] Cf. my article in the *Review of Politics,* V (July, 1943), 275-301 and in *The Catholic Historical Review,* XXXI (July, 1945), 133-53. [Father Isaac Hecker, an American-born convert to Roman Catholicism and an associate of Orestes Brownson (cf. n. 30), was a staunch exponent of a program for rapid cultural adaptation for the immigrant Roman Catholics. He was convinced that a Roman Catholic could be an equally good American citizen. In 1891, three years after his death, his biography was translated into French. The translation was so poorly done that Father Hecker was attacked in France for heretical views which he never taught. Pope Leo XIII took notice of the controversy and in 1899 condemned five points which he termed "False Americanism": (1) an overemphasis on the direct influence of the Holy Spirit to the detriment of ecclesiastical spiritual direction; (2) the exaltation of natural virtues above the supernatural; (3) an overemphasis on religious activism to the exclusion of humility, charity, and obedience; (4) the rejection of religious vows; (5) untested and dubious methods of evangelism. Since no one in America held these positions the papal condemnation has been characterized as "hardly more than hypothetical," and had the effect of "making sure that such erroneous opinions would never arise in this country." See Theodore Maynard, "The American Heresy," chap. 25 of *The Story of American Catholicism* (New York: The Macmillan Company, 1954), pp. 498-521.—ED.]

gencies among American Catholics on such questions as th application of Gregory XVI's condemnation of the slav trade,[2] the timeliness of the declaration of papal infall bility,[3] or the extent of the papal condemnation of secr societies,[4] but there has been no difference on the essentia doctrines involved in these disputes. In startling contrast t this unity in dogma and morals has been the extreme diver gence among American Catholics in political beliefs and i economic and social status. What there is of a distinctiv Catholic culture is the result of the interaction between th doctrinal unity and this political, social, and economic di vergence. It took its dominant form during the stormy year immediately before the Civil War.

In matters of theology the historian has little difficulty i determining the American Catholic position. The doctrina uniformity can be ascribed to several sources such as th fact that the church in the United States took form afte the great theological controversies of western Europe, tha the American people have been so completely absorbed witl the practical problems of settling an unconquered countr that they are not accustomed to theological speculations and that the Catholic immigrants have been mostly down trodden and persecuted peoples who have clung unques tioningly to their religious faith as their chief hope in tim of trial. One should also remember that the existing separa tion of Church and State has eliminated the chief sponso of heretical and dogmatic divisions—political interference

---

[2] Madeleine Hooke Rice, *American Catholic Opinion in the Slavery Con troversy* (New York: Columbia University Press, 1944), pp. 62-72.

[3] Raymond J. Clancy, C.S.C., "American Catholic Prelates in the Vatica Council" in *United States Catholic History Records & Studies*, XXVII 8-135.

[4] F. J. Zwierlein, *The Life and Letters of Bishop McQuaid* (3 vols. Rochester, N. Y.: The Art Print Shop, 1926), II, 378-474, and Fergu Macdonald, C.P., *The Catholic Church and the Secret Societies in th United States* (New York: The United States Historical Society, 1946) especially chap. 6.

Some disciplinary problems among the American Catholics arose as soon as these immigrants began to enjoy the freedom of the United States, but the scandals resulting from undisciplined clergymen and lay trusteeism[5] had been reduced to a minimum before the greater growth of Catholicism began. By 1829, the date of the first Provincial Council of Baltimore, dogmatic and disciplinary uniformity had been established in nearly all details. Later councils merely confirmed and developed these foundations. Catholics of all political parties, despite wide differences of economic and social status and of national origins, have quickly rallied to the defense of the common faith just as they have rallied to the defense of American social and political institutions. In all these diverse kinds of Catholic citizens there has developed a common element, founded upon their religious faith and the common loyalty to the American state yet embracing all these differences, which can be called an American Catholic culture. That this culture has not been as perfect as it might be is a matter of common observation. In most critical judgments, Catholic educational institutions[6] have been made to carry most of the blame for this low cultural level, but in so judging the critics have shown little understanding of the factors of peasant origins and frontier handicaps which have been almost insuperable obstacles to the success of Catholic education.

Roughly, all American cultural ideals are compounded

[5] ["Trusteeism" is the name applied to the attempts of laymen serving as trustees of Roman Catholic parishes to assume control over such matters as finances, properties, and the appointment and dismissal of priests, powers which the Roman Catholic Church reserves to the hierarchy. In 1805 Bishop John Carroll won a court verdict against the trustees of St. John's Church, Baltimore; in 1822 Pope Pius VII condemned "trusteeism"; and the Supreme Court closed the battle in 1842 by refusing to review a decision against the trustees of St. Louis' Cathedral in New Orleans.—ED.]

[6] James M. Campbell, "The Catholic Contribution to the American College" in *Vital Problems in Catholic Education in the United States*, ed. Roy J. Deferrari (Washington: Catholic University of America Press, 1939), pp. 84-107.

of two elements, the European traditions brought by the immigrant and the effects of the American frontier—in broad sense of the term—on these immigrants. American Catholic culture has been no exception to the process but the history of the Catholic minority differs from that of the Protestant majority's groups because the Catholic immigrants have been overwhelmingly non-English. American Catholic culture has undergone a series of rises and declines under the effect of successive waves of non-English migrations and has not completely solved the problems of its later immigrants even today. Yet, the essential characteristics of American Catholic culture were determined by the generation of Catholics in America during the great immigration from 1830 to the Civil War. Unwittingly the nativistic and anti-Catholic reaction[7] of the eighteen-forties and fifties furnished the hammer and the anvil by which this distinctive Catholic cultural unity was created; and this cultural unity has slowly absorbed all the later immigrations since the Civil War.

In most of the historical accounts of the Catholic body in the United States the cultural composition of the group has been generally misunderstood. No one, for example, has explained why the cultural and social position of English-speaking Catholics before 1835 was higher than it has ever been since that time. Some writers do not recognize the existence of the group before the eighteen-thirties. Be-

[7] [The rapid growth of the Roman Catholic group in the middle years of the nineteenth century incited fear and suspicion among some Protestants. Organizations such as the American Protestant Association, the Order of the Star-Spangled Banner, the Native American Party, and the Masonic Order led the attack on the Roman Catholics. The Know-Nothing Party, an anti-Roman Catholic political party, had temporary success in state elections in 1854 and 1855 but declined and disappeared after failing badly in the national election of 1856. The American Protective Association renewed the attack in the late 1880's, as did the Ku Klux Klan in the late 1920's. See Ray A. Billington, *The Protestant Crusade, 1820-1860* (New York: The Macmillan Company, 1933) and John Higham, *Strangers in the Land: Patterns of American Nativism, 1860-1925* (New Brunswick, N. J.: Rutgers University Press, 1955) for full accounts.—ED.]

ause the Catholic body achieved national importance only when the number of Catholics had been suddenly swollen by Irish and German immigration in the second quarter of the nineteenth century, most historians of American social and cultural life have tended to classify Catholicism as a foreign importation,[8] almost out of harmony with the dominant Anglo-American culture. This is understandable, for no one can deny that the dominant American culture is actually English and Protestant, although greatly modified by the frontier and by American experience. The supposition that American culture is essentially Protestant, however, overlooks the fact that since 1634, at least, there has always been an English Catholic minority, truly Catholic and truly American according to the times, within the present United States. That minority has always accepted all the essentials of English culture while remaining loyal to their Catholic faith. The members of this Anglo-American Catholic group were never very numerous. They were scarcely thirty thousand in three million in 1790,[9] but they were accepted as fully American, even though their faith was not approved. This Catholic minority of Maryland and Pennsylvania had absorbed many non-English Catholics even before the Revolution without changing its character, because these earlier Irish, German, and French immigrants had adopted generally the cultural standards of the English Catholics and were quite indistinguishable from them after a generation in the United States.

The number of Irish, French, and German immigrants in this Anglo-American Catholic minority prior to 1820

[8] Cf. Merle Curti, *The Growth of American Thought* (New York: Harper & Bros., 1943), pp. 316 f., 492 f.

[9] Sister Mary Augustina Ray, B.V.M., *American Opinion of Roman Catholics in the Eighteenth Century* (New York: Columbia University Press, 1936) traces the decline of political opposition to Catholicism under the influence of the Revolution and the granting of political toleration; cf. especially pp. 292 f.

actually was scarcely greater in relation to the English Catholics than the non-English immigrants were in relation to the total English population of the country during this early period. The relation of the Anglo-American Catholic group towards the non-Catholic majority, on the other hand, can be described roughly as the relation of the Catholic minority in England towards the English majority, minus the legal disabilities of English Catholics. Since the Gunpowder Plot in 1605, Catholics in England[10] had ceased to hope for a corporate reunion of England with the Church of Rome. They bore as best they could the social and economic persecution which cut more deeply than the political disbarment, and saw their numbers frequently lessened—before the Oxford revival—by the usual wearing away at the edges of Catholics whose faith had weakened under the strain. Nevertheless, English Catholics remained loyal to their country as well as to their Catholic friends and sought to attain the position of a select cultured minority. American Catholics before 1820, however, had higher hopes than English Catholics because they had attained equality before the law and because they had been reenforced especially by a group of cultured French priests who had fled into exile from the persecution of the French Revolution.

A second and perhaps more important reason for the usual misinterpretation of the cultural relation between the Catholic minority and the majority group in the United States has been the insistence of certain Catholic historians, particularly John Gilmary Shea[11] and Monsignor Peter Guil-

---

[10] David Mathew, *The Jacobean Age* (New York: Longmans, Green & Co., 1938), pp. 11-16; also Philip Hughes, *The Catholic Question* (New York: Sheed & Ward, 1929), pp. 122-41.

[11] John G. Shea in *The History of the Catholic Church within the United States* (4 vols.; New York: J. G. Shea, 1886-92) is less given to this devotion to the Irish immigrants than Monsignor Guilday because of his adherence to a more strictly hierarchical history and because of his broader perspective.

ay,[12] on identifying the Irish Catholic with the Catholic minority chiefly because the more numerous Irish spoke English and had adopted the United States as their country once they had landed. Such a theory, which was apparently accepted by many Irish Catholic leaders a hundred years ago, will hold in the political sphere but culturally overlooks completely the difference between English and Irish cultural ideals in the nineteenth century. It also ignores the existence of the definite Anglo-American Catholic minority in that early period. This viewpoint too hastily considered all opposition to the Irish immigrant to be based on religious belief alone. Actually the continued existence and growth of the Anglo-American Catholic group in the larger Catholic group is the chief connecting link between the history of the Catholic immigrant and that of the native Protestant and is the basic element in our distinctive American Catholic culture.

In American ecclesiastical history of the first two decades of the nineteenth century the existence of a number of French clerical exiles and their opposition to the immigrant Irish clergyman has been a source of confusion in evaluating the Catholic group of the period. These French clergy have been accused of plotting a Gallic domination of the American Church, where they were actually defenders of the Anglo-American group against an Irish invasion. It was understandable that these Irish immigrants of the day, especially the clergy, regarded themselves as more American than the French who spoke only broken and accented English. But it must be borne in mind that in the broader

---

[12] Cf. Patrick K. Guilday, *The Catholic Church in Virginia (1815-1822)* (New York: The United States Catholic Historical Society, 1924) and *The Life and Times of John England, First Bishop of Charleston, 1786-1842* (2 vols.; New York: The American Press, 1927). The otherwise very careful Monsignor is quite explicit in these matters in his "Introduction" to the latter study (pp. 1-35) and in Vol. II (pp. 68-110).

American scene the French Huguenots, such as the Jay
the Faneuils, the Legarés, and the Pettigrues, and the Swi
Albert Gallatin, were accepted as part of the majority grou
without too much objection. And the Catholic French clerg
men were readily received by the Anglo-American Catholi
and even by the American non-Catholics because of the
learning and culture. Abbé Jean Cheverus and Abbé Franc.
Matignon[13] were revered by the New England Yankees wh
despised the Irish immigrant, and Abbé Jean Dubois i
Virginia and Abbé Gabriel Richard in Michigan were ac
cepted as honorable citizens. The sympathy of these Frenc
priests was naturally with the native Americans with whom
they generally associated, especially those of some socia
position. The Irish[14] on the contrary were generally antago
nistic toward the English, had even lost most of the tradi
tions of ancient Irish culture, and had little social position
The French clergymen, particularly Archbishop Ambros
Maréchal of Baltimore, looked upon the Irish as just a
much foreigners as themselves and wanted the control o
the clergy in the hands of American clergymen. Further
their antagonism toward some of the Irish clergy was based
upon several cases of clerical disobedience and misconduct
Actually, most of our knowledge of the Catholic minorit
at this time arises from the troubles between the French
archbishop and his Irish suffragans, but these troubles ar
symbolic of the cultural conflict within the Catholic grou
of that time.

[13] R. H. Lord, J. E. Sexton, and E. T. Harrington, *History of the Arch
diocese of Boston* (3 vols.; New York: Sheed & Ward, 1944), I, 619-31

[14] The best account of the Irish immigrants of this period is that o
W. F. Adams, *Ireland and Irish Emigration to the New World from 1815
to the Famine* (New Haven: Yale University Press, 1932), especially chap
7, "The Fruits of Emigration." Noteworthy on the cultural conflict is M. L
Hansen's essay "Immigration and Puritanism" in *The Immigrant in Ameri
can History* (Cambridge: Harvard University Press, 1940), pp. 97-128
Cf. also, J. A. Krout and D. R. Fox, *The Completion of Independence
(New York: The Macmillan Company, 1944), pp. 377 ff.

Partly, perhaps, because the Irish were the most active Catholics in the English-speaking world and partly because of some ecclesiastical intrigue in Rome, the Sacred Congregation of the Propaganda had been prevailed upon to appoint several Irish bishops to the American episcopate, thus giving the new Irish immigrants spokesmen for their opinions in the government of American Catholics. Father John Connolly, O.P., of Ireland was named bishop of New York in 1815, and Fathers Henry Conwell, Patrick Kelly, and John England, also from Ireland, were named to the sees of Philadelphia, Richmond, and Charleston, respectively. None of these men had even been in the United States before their appointment and all had been elected without any recommendation from the American bishops. Archbishop Maréchal was alarmed at this action. He had proposed American-born Benedict Fenwick for Charleston and wanted either men experienced in America or, perhaps, Englishmen[15] appointed to the other sees. He began at once to petition the Sacred Congregation against further appointments without the consultation of the American bishops. To Maréchal the increasing Irish immigration and the growth in the number of Irish priests and bishops constituted the first threat of a real foreign domination of the American church, and he felt called upon by his position to prevent such a situation. To the Irish, however, the activities of Maréchal and the other French clergymen looked rather like an attempt at Gallic domination. The care of the Anglo-American Catholics as such and the promotion of their interests seem to have rested mostly with the French clergymen since the natives had not produced enough native priests to care for their own needs.

Bishop John England, the foremost of the new Irish clergymen, was undoubtedly an outstanding ecclesiastic

---

[15] Guilday, *The Life and Times of John England, op. cit.*, I, 251 f.

9

possessing exceptional gifts as an orator and as a journali[
Despite the fact that he was situated in a diocese containi
few Catholics and away from the other Catholic cente
he began at once to influence the whole Catholic minori
He visited other Catholic congregations along the coast a
in 1822 founded the first really Catholic newspaper in t
United States, the *U. S. Catholic Miscellany,* for the expo
tion of the Catholic faith. He so delighted Catholics a
non-Catholics by his oratory as to receive countless invit
tions to speak to American audiences throughout the cou
try—once speaking before the Congress of the United State
Although Bishop England had been an outstanding Iri
nationalist as a clergyman and editor in Ireland, he becam
an honest, zealous American as soon as he arrived in th
country. If he seemed extremely pro-Irish in his activities
was because he felt that the Irish were the chief Catholi
in the English-speaking world, European or American, an
were being attacked chiefly because of their faith. He an
his fellow Irish immigrants accepted American citizenshi
and considered themselves entitled to all American soci
privileges as well. Actually, he and his confreres from Ir
land were not as much a part of the American Catholi
group as the French-speaking Maréchal and the Frenc
Sulpicians of St. Mary's Seminary in Baltimore. In the col
umns of the *Miscellany*[16] even England admitted that th
Irish immigrants were not all the social equals of the olde
English inhabitants of the country. He had, however, n
great respect for the culture of the French archbishop and
his Sulpician associates who, he maintained, would neve
be accepted by Americans because of their foreign languag
and accent.[17]

In the 1820's when England insisted that Maréchal call a

[16] *U.S. Catholic Miscellany,* Aug. 3, 1825, p. 80.
[17] *Ibid.,* Sept. 14, 1825, pp. 5 f.

provincial council to lay down rules for the trustee problems and for other difficulties, Maréchal rightly understood that he could scarcely hope to control the discussions in such an assembly against these new Irish appointees. To England's request he answered[18] that the disciplinary troubles were purely local and that there were no new dogmatic or moral problems needing conciliar definition. At the same time, Bishop England, noting the lack of clergymen, proposed a scheme for recruiting clerical candidates from Ireland, with special arrangements to eliminate unruly candidates. But to this proposal also, Maréchal turned a deaf ear. While Maréchal did seem to look down on the Irish clergymen, so many of whom were causing disciplinary problems in New York, Philadelphia, Norfolk, and Charleston, there is another explanation for his action besides racial and national prejudice. Not even England could deny that most of the rebellious clergymen of the day were Irish. Further, there existed in the newly-arrived Irish immigrants a confusion of Irish nationalism and Catholicism in their public utterances, notably in their newspapers.[19] Nor was the cultural level of the Irish flock as high as the Anglo-American Catholic group. Consequently Maréchal could justly feel that to place the control of the growing Catholic body in the hands of such a group would endanger the future of the American Church. He wanted a "national clergy."[20]

Maréchal first begged Rome to check any further Euro-

[18] First draft of a letter of Maréchal to England, July 28, 1821, in the Baltimore Papers, University of Notre Dame Archives.

[19] This confusion of religion and nationality is clearly demonstrated in the first issue of *The Freeman's Journal* (July 4, 1840). Other examples can be found elsewhere in that newspaper as well as in *The Truth Teller* (New York, 1825-55), *The Pilot* (Boston, 1846-), and *The American Celt* (1852-57). The *U.S. Catholic Miscellany,* while manifesting deep interest in Irish news, was notably American and theological, as was also *The Catholic Telegraph* (1831-) of Cincinnati.

[20] Manuscript of a sermon preached by Maréchal, Dec. 20, 1817, in St. Peter's Church in Baltimore in which he summarizes the condition of the church in America at the beginning of his episcopate. University of Notre Dame Archives.

pean intrigue in the appointment of American bishops. He sought and finally obtained the nomination of episcopal candidates by the American hierarchy. This he hoped would prevent the appointment of bishops who would be totally unacquainted with the American scene. In his own nominations he usually recommended American or English candidates but did prefer the Irish Franciscan Maguire for the proposed see of Pittsburgh over the Frenchman Stephen Theodore Badin on one occasion.[21] He did succeed in having the English-born James Whitfield appointed his coadjutor and successor and backed Maryland-born Benedict Fenwick for several sees, finally succeeding in having him named to the see of Boston. Whitfield, carrying on the tradition, was in turn succeeded by the American-born and Sulpician-trained Samuel Eccleston. Thus for another generation the archiepiscopal see remained in the possession of the Anglo-American Catholics. But the rising generation of American Catholics was dominantly Irish in numbers, especially near the ports of entry and in the mill towns. The newer bishops, nominated by the existing hierarchy, continued to be Sulpician-trained, but were becoming more and more of Irish descent. Nevertheless the cultural leaven of the Catholic congregations remained the Anglo-American group which alone had social position. These Anglo-American Catholics were to a great extent rural, and even partially western, as, for example, the Bardstown group of transplanted Marylanders which prospered and spread about the Middle West.

Maréchal never called a provincial assembly of the bishops, but after his death Bishop England succeeded in having Rome order the Provincial Councils of 1829 and 1833. As Maréchal had foreseen, England dominated these assemblies and spoke the mind of the hierarchy in the pastoral letters

---

[21] Derived from the small manuscript volume "Letters of Some Importance" containing copies of some of Maréchal's letters in his own hand. University of Notre Dame Archives.

12

to the clergy and laity.[22] But England's influence was checked. Even his Charleston diocese could not support the cultural institutions he planned. Likewise, other bishops found that the immigrants could not support colleges and seminaries. To make cultural matters worse for the Catholic groups, even the faculty of Mount St. Mary's College, at Emmitsburg, Maryland, the most promising cultural institution, was sacrificed to make bishops for the expanding church.

During the decade after 1833, increasing Irish immigration continued and the French clergy were not renewed in proportionate numbers. The native and Anglo-American group were not numerous enough to supply clergy for the invading thousands. Some Belgian, German, French, and Italian priests were obtained, but the greater number of the new clergymen were Irish or the sons of Irish immigrants. It was a natural consequence of this large number of Irish faithful and Irish clergymen that the chief candidates for episcopal honors in the growing Catholic Church in the United States during the eighteen-thirties and forties should have come from these Irish immigrants, although years of service and even training in the country were prerequisites for these promotions. Father Francis Patrick Kenrick,[23] after twelve years in the frontier seminary of Bardstown, Kentucky, became coadjutor to Bishop Henry Conwell in Philadelphia. Father John B. Purcell[24] had risen to the presidency

---

[22] "The Pastoral Letter of 1837" written by England contains an extensive defense of the Catholic immigrant without any recognition of the native Catholics. *The National Pastorals of the American Hierarchy (1792-1919)*, ed. Patrick K. Guilday (Washington: National Catholic Welfare Conference, 1923), pp. 90 ff.

[23] John J. O'Shea, *The Two Archbishops Kenrick* (Philadelphia: John J. McVey, 1904) is very unsatisfactory. The forthcoming study of Francis Patrick Kenrick by Rev. Hugh Nolan will cover the years before his promotion to Baltimore in 1851 [Hugh Nolan, *Francis Patrick Kenrick* (Washington: The Catholic University of America Press, 1949).—ED.]

[24] There is no satisfactory study of Purcell. The unfortunate financial scandal of his last years as archbishop has clouded over an earlier life of great missionary zeal in the Ohio valley.

of Mount St. Mary's College before he was appointed to the western see of Cincinnati. Father John Hughes[25] had come to the United States as a young man, had received his training in this country, and served with Bishop Francis Kenrick in Philadelphia. Father Peter Richard Kenrick had served in his brother's diocese of Philadelphia before being named coadjutor to Bishop Joseph Rosati in St. Louis. The German immigration into the Ohio Valley also received recognition in 1844 with the appointment of Father John Martin Henni, the editor of the German Catholic newspaper *Wahrheitsfreund,* as the first Bishop of Milwaukee. Father Anthony Blanc, after twelve years in Louisiana, became the bishop of the French at New Orleans. Father John Timon in the new see of Buffalo, Father Richard Vincent Whelan of Richmond and Wheeling, Father Ignatius Reynolds of Charleston, Father John J. Chanche of Natchez, and, later, Father John McGill of Richmond, together with Samuel Eccleston in Baltimore and Benedict Fenwick in Boston of the older group, continued for a time to carry on the Anglo-American tradition in the American hierarchy. None of these bishops was an outstanding public figure. The real leadership in the Catholic hierarchy was supplied by the more active Irish-born prelates of whom John Purcell of Cincinnati seemed nearest to being a member of the old English Catholic group,[26] perhaps because he had more fully experienced the leveling influence of the frontier. Outside of the ports of entry he was the chief American prelate,

[25] A biography of Archbishop Hughes was begun by Monsignor Peter K. Guilday and was continued by Thomas F. O'Connor and Henry Browne, but has not been revised for publication. The biographies of J. R. G. Hassard (New York: D. Appleton and Company, 1866) and Henry Brann (New York: Dodd, Mead and Company, 1892) are inadequate.

[26] Purcell's Americanization had been so complete that Bishop Ignatius Reynolds once apologized to him for a remark Reynolds had made against foreign-born bishops in the presence of Purcell, whom he had come to look upon as a native. Letter of Reynolds to Purcell, Sept. 27, 1847, University of Notre Dame Archives.

uilding up a notable church organization in the Middle
West, which combined the older English Catholic pioneers,
remnants of the French, the numerous German immigrants,
and the Irish who had followed the canals and railroads
into the interior of the country. But even Purcell was Irish-
born.

Meanwhile, as a result of the heavy Irish and German
immigration between 1830 and 1850, the Catholic group in
the United States had become overwhelmingly immigrant,
chiefly Irish in the eastern cities and German in the settlements in the Middle West. The violence of the nativistic
reaction continued. In vain the American Bishops Timon,
McGill, and Whelan sought a native American for the position of Archbishop of Baltimore when Samuel Eccleston
died in 1851.[27] Their only candidates were Chanche and
Timon who did not compare in ability to the Irish-born
prelates. Rome, at the request of most of the American
bishops, named Francis Patrick Kenrick of Philadelphia to
the Baltimore see. Thus, when the first Plenary Council of
Baltimore was convened in 1852, the American hierarchy
consisted of six foreign-born archbishops and seventeen
foreign-born bishops. There were no American-born archbishops and only nine of the bishops had been born in the
United States. The chief archiepiscopal sees—New York,
Baltimore, Cincinnati, and St. Louis—were occupied by prelates of Irish birth. In point of fact this Irish domination
represented the numerical composition of the Catholic body
at this time. Of the Catholic population, those in New

[27] Letter of Bishop Richard V. Whelan of Wheeling to Bishop John Mc-
Gill of Richmond, May 15, 1851, Richmond Diocesan Archives. The New
York *Times* of July 31 and August 1, 1854, contained editorials referring
to Brownson's articles and hinting that there existed dissensions between
the native and foreign-born prelates in the church. This was denied by
Hughes under the pen name "Philo-Veritas." (Cf. *Freeman's Journal,* Aug.
9, 1854.) Hughes was correct in stating there were no serious differences
between the two groups of prelates and he may have been unaware of the
feeling of such bishops as Whelan and Reynolds.

15

England and the Middle Atlantic states were almost solid Irish and were in control of nearly all the Catholic pres The English Catholics who had increased only by conve sions and by natural growth were chiefly in the upp South although many groups of them had gone to vario farming regions in the Ohio valley. The German Cathol immigrants were increasing rapidly in the North Centr states but because of language difficulties exerted little i fluence on the general Catholic body.

This change in the hierarchy to Irish domination did n imply any political maneuvers by the Irish or other foreig born ecclesiastics. The bishops were rightly chosen from th more capable of the clergy in the field and were the nom nees of the other bishops both native and foreign-bor There was already some discussion of the need of separa organizations for the German faithful, who did not spea English, but Archbishop Cajetan Bedini,[28] the papal lega who visited the country in 1853, disapproved of such separation.

There was, however, an increase in the number of Germa bishops. Altogether, then, the change in the hierarchy a tually represented the change in the cultural and natur origins of the Catholic population. The cultural unity o the Catholic minority before 1830 was gradually reestab lished on the foundations of the common faith and sacra ments, but, while the English and native-born Catholic provided the cultural leadership, the numerical predomi nance of the immigrant group had changed the quality an character of the whole group.

There are few manifestations of strictly cultural characte by which one can estimate the cultural accomplishments o

---

[28] John G. Shea, *op. cit.,* III, 364 f. Bedini urged the appointment o more American-born bishops whom he found "more courageous and fea less, more steadfast in the struggles which not infrequently arise."

the Catholic group of that day. Outside of a few converts there were few writers or thinkers of note.[29] The Catholic lawyers such as Roger Taney and William Read of Maryland and the Spaldings and Elders of Kentucky were examples of the continued growth of the Anglo-American Catholic group throughout the period. It is also significant that even the immigrants looked to these border states for leadership concerning Catholic opinions on the great national problems of the day. Orestes Brownson[30] and other Yankee converts could complain of this but they actually preferred that leadership in most affairs to dictation from the immigrant. The oratory and the Catholic press of the eastern cities were on a much lower cultural plane and were devoted to political rather than to cultural pursuits. Numerically the Catholic population was chiefly in the ports of entry and the mill towns of the North. These northern Catholics, however, were mostly poor immigrants struggling for a livelihood in the less desirable section of the towns and buffeted by the storms of nativism. Naturally their pastors were gravely concerned with their welfare and defended them not in literary journals but in the press and from pulpit and platforms. In the New York area, Catholic leadership in public affairs had passed into the hands of Bishop Hughes, whose diocese became the center of most

---

[29] This is clearly brought out in the essay "Catholic Literature in the United States" in *The Metropolitan* (Baltimore) II (1854), 69-75; 133-39; 198-204.

[30] [Orestes Brownson was converted to Roman Catholicism in 1844 after a spiritual and philosophical pilgrimage which took him successively through Presbyterianism, New England liberalism, Universalism, and Unitarianism. He became an ardent exponent of Roman Catholicism in the United States and championed the effort to free it from the charge of being an immigrant church and the related "nativist" opposition. He wanted the immigrant Roman Catholics to adjust to American culture as rapidly as possible. His approach and program were opposed both within and outside of the Catholic Church (cf. pp. 22, 24 f. below). Theodore Maynard, *Orestes Brownson, Yankee Radical, Catholic* (New York: The Macmillan Company, 1943) is a standard biography.—ED.]

of the public controversy. Closely associated with him in this work were Bishop Kenrick in Philadelphia and Bishop Fenwick and later Bishop Fitzpatrick in Boston; but no other prelate commanded the attention of the Irish immigrant and the American public as easily as Bishop Hughes. In him the Irish immigrant group found its cleverest and most potent expression. He sought to protect the immigrants from the nativists and to direct their efforts for their own good. He exerted this protection chiefly in the fields of politics and oratory where the impoverished immigrant could best be marshaled. He saved his flock from physical persecution in the riots of 1844[31] but he kept them in the cities where progress and cultural development for the lower classes came with more difficulty.[32] In general, the Catholic bishops were conspicuously absent in the movement against slavery, the temperance movement, and in the other social reforms of the day. They could not concern themselves with these things as long as their flocks lacked religious care and economic security.

Considering the poverty of most of the Catholic immigrants it is easy to see that the chief burden of the Catholic clergy during the three decades before the Civil War was not to build up universities or other institutions of higher culture. They were absorbed in the immediate task of giving the sacraments and essential Catholic instruction to these impoverished immigrants and of protecting them as far as

[31] [Vehement attacks by nativist groups on Roman Catholicism as un-American and dangerous to American religious and political ideals and institutions led to a series of anti-Catholic riots between 1834 and 1844. The worst riots took place in Philadelphia in May and July, 1844. Two Roman Catholic churches were burned, others were defaced and sacked, a convent and entire blocks of Irish Catholic homes were burned, thirteen people were killed and more than fifty wounded. See Billington, *op. cit.,* "The Philadelphia Riots of 1844," pp. 220-37.—Ed.]

[32] Cf. *The Metropolitan* (Baltimore), IV, 251-53. The letter of "Oliver" on the Buffalo Convention of 1856 for the promotion of Irish colonization in the west shows that some at least disagreed with Hughes.

ossible from the fury of the nativistic movement.[33] That his nativism was to a great extent a religious persecution amply proven in the controversial literature of the day. But at the same time it was a cultural reaction to the influx of immigrants. As long as the dominant cultural group was so hostile to the Catholic Church it is understandable that the defenders of the Irish immigrants were the Catholic clergy and that Bishop (Archbishop after 1850) Hughes and his fellow bishops should object to the efforts of Orestes Brownson and other native American Catholics to produce harmony between the immigrant Catholics and the nativists. Indeed, for the Irish immigrant who had fled from English oppression, the combination of religious and political persecution was not new. He was not surprised to find the English descendant in America attempting to carry on the same persecution but he did appeal to his rights as guaranteed by American law. In his appeal to the law the immigrant was sustained, but socially and culturally there remained a division between the immigrant and the nativist which only generations of living together could overcome.

The native-born Catholics, including the older Irish, looked forward to the day when the immigrant would cease to be looked upon as a foreigner. Brownson, a militant Yankee, wanted to eliminate this distinction at once.[34] Archbishop Hughes objected to Brownson's reasonings because he feared that a hasty adoption of American ways would result in a loss in faith outweighing any social gain. Later on the Americanized Irish would use the Brownson argu-

---

[33] The Bishop's Pastoral Letter of 1852 stressed the great material handicap involved in caring for these poorer immigrants in estimating the future prospects of the Catholic Church in the country. *The National Pastorals of the American Hierarchy (1792-1919),* ed. Patrick K. Guilday (Washington: National Catholic Welfare Conference, 1923), pp. 187-91.

[34] Brownson's more notable essays on this topic are in the *Brownson Quarterly Review* (New York), XI (January, 1854), 1-29; XI (July, 1854), 328-53; XI (October, 1854), 447-86; XIV (January, 1857) 114-41).

ment against the Germans, Poles, and French Canadian. In the case of the Irish immigrant, the absence of a language difficulty did not prevent Archbishop Hughes from realizing that there was a cultural difference between the immigrants and the native Americans.[35] But like the defenders of later national groups he failed to see the advantage of more rapid Americanization. The cultural conflict in the eighteen-forties and fifties, as had been anticipated by Marechal, was the first great manifestation of a foreign nationalism in the American church. Culturally the policy of Hughes set back the progress of the Irish immigrant at least a generation, as such policies have set back other Catholic groups wherever they have manifested themselves. In some instances, it is true, the opposition to the immigrant of the earlier period included local political feeling because the immigrant had become the tool of politicians;[36] there was, also, some economic feeling manifested by the incipient labor unions against foreign labor competition. These latter however, were minor items in a struggle that was mainly religious and cultural.

Since the cultural opposition to the Irish immigrant during the second quarter of the nineteenth century was chiefly on religious grounds, it was to the religious advantage of the Catholic group that the clerical leaders who defended the immigrant were men from Catholic countries where no compromise in religious matters was the order of the day. In the Catholic unity moulded by the nativistic opposition,

[35] In his "Lecture on the Present Condition and Prospects of the Catholic Church in the United States," in *The Complete Works of the Most Rev. John Hughes, D.D., Archbishop of New York. Comprising his sermons, letters, lectures, speeches, etc. Carefully compiled and edited from the best sources*, comp. and ed. Laurence Kehoe (2 vols.; New York: The American News Co., 1864-65, or The Catholic Publication House, 1964). Hughes distinguishes the original Maryland group, the immigrants and the converts in the growth of the Catholic Church in this country.

[36] Oscar Handlin, *Boston's Immigrants 1790-1865* (Cambridge: Harvard University Press, 1941), stresses this political backwardness but shows a serious lack of appreciation for the religious faith of the immigrants.

merican Catholicism acquired a new aggressive character-
tic. Even though the more dominant immigrant groups
ere of a lower strain culturally, their staunch defense of
eir religion created in this country the most militant Cath-
ic organization in the English-speaking world. Before this
ange the Anglo-American Catholics, like their English
rethren, did not show themselves active apologists of the
atholic position, and in striving to advance the faith by
atholic preeminence in cultural matters they had continued
e defeatist attitude of the English minority group of colo-
ial days. The Irish and German Catholic leaders, who
ere unaccustomed to making any compromises in their re-
tions with non-Catholics, insisted instead on their full
ghts in all public matters. The position of Bishop Francis
atrick Kenrick in Philadelphia and of Bishop John Hughes
 New York on the public schools and on the use of the
atholic Bible in those schools may be open to question on
e grounds of strategy[37] but the uncompromising defense
f their flocks by these bishops was in the best Catholic tra-
ition. Since that time American Catholicism has never re-
eated to the position of a defeatist minority. Nevertheless,
ecause the opposition to the immigrants was based on
ore than religious disagreements, there were bound to be
ome differences within the ranks of the Catholic reaction
 the nativistic movement.

Bishops Hughes and Kenrick were not native Americans
nd represented the immigrant point of view in the public
iscussions, and the circumstances of the times would not
llow any public manifestations of a different point of view
y the native-born bishops. Yet there has always been some
ativism among the American Catholics. Their patriotism
ould have no other results, although Hughes and other

[37] Ray A. Billington, *op. cit*, especially chapter 12, "The Catholic Church
lunders," pp. 289-321. Billington considers this aggressiveness a blunder.

episcopal defenders of the immigrants failed to understa
that even a Catholic could resent the immigrant invasi
Brownson, as he showed in his *Review*,[38] felt strongly t
Yankee resentment towards the immigrant and, in Lo
siana, Abbé Adrien Rouquett[39] expressed in French poe
an Americanism that opposed the Irish immigrants and l
him to associate with the American Party. And there w
other manifestations of this internal cultural conflict in t
Catholic group.

Perhaps the locality where the amalgamation of th
cultural strains into an American Catholic culture can
most clearly observed was the Middle Western frontier
There the immigrant groups living away from the cit
yielded more quickly to the general cultural trends. At le
the Catholics in these western settlements—if we except t
German mass colonies which were comparable to the Ir
groups in the cities—were quickly Americanized. It w
noted by the early missionaries in the Middle West th
there was less bigotry on the frontier as long as the comm
problem of conquering the wilderness and the prairies ga
little occasion for internecine cultural differences. General
the bigotry that appeared on the frontier was an import

[38] There are several rough drafts of Brownson letters supporting his po
tion on this point in the Brownson MSS, University of Notre Da
Archives.

[39] D. R. Lebreton, *Chata-Ima, The Life of Adrien-Emmanuel Rouque*
(Baton Rouge: Louisiana State University Press, 1947), pp. 187-98.

[40] A capable study of this Kentucky group after 1815 and its filial sett
ments in the neighboring states has not been made. Sister M. Ramc
Mattingly's *The Catholic Church on the Kentucky Frontier (1785-181*
(Washington: Catholic University of America Press, 1937) does not cov
this later period. M. J. Spaulding's *Sketches of the Early Catholic Missio
of Kentucky* (Louisville: B. J. Webb and Brother, 1844) and *Sketches
the Life and Times and Character of Benedict J. Flaget* (Louisville: We
& Levering, 1852) are based on material that has since disappeared. B.
Webb's *The Centenary of Catholicity in Kentucky* (Louisville: C. A. Roge
1884) is informative about many things but is incomplete and disorganize
Many private genealogical studies are being prepared about these Kentuc
families.

tion from the older settlements, deliberately propagated by missionary societies.[41]

The Americanization of the immigrant Catholic away from the concentration on the seaboard is shown best in the Kentucky Catholic group which was augmented by Catholics of other nationalities as it spread across the Ohio and Mississippi to found new centers of settlement. These frontiersmen were joined by Irish canal and railroad workers and by German farmers. These English Catholic families— many dating their arrival back to 1681 in Maryland—built up first the Kentucky communities of Bardstown, Loretto, Holy Cross, and the like with Catholic colleges and a seminary, three communities of religious women, and a Dominican monastery. Many of these families, such as the Spaldings, Wathens, Coomes, Haydens, Clements, and Mattinglys, remained in Kentucky, some at Bardstown and others in more prosperous communities. The same families are also found in Daviess County, Indiana, and in early Catholic communities at Paris, Illinois, and Lancaster, Ohio, and in Tennessee and Missouri. They have given to the Catholic Church many bishops and priests and prominent lawyers and physicians. Sometimes when they moved into less Catholic communities they achieved positions of local importance, although the propaganda of the anti-Catholic movements of the eighteen-forties and fifties usually prevented this. In most communities where Catholics lived, the church or mission chapel with a pastor of almost any national origin was the center of a growing Catholic culture. Usually the Anglo-American element furnished the social leadership of the group and frequently a professional vocation; to this

[41] Cf. Thomas T. McAvoy, *The Catholic Church in Indiana 1789-1834* (New York: Columbia University Press, 1940), pp. 126 ff., 141 f., 158 f., 200 f.; also George M. Stephenson, "Nativism in the Forties and Fifties, with Special Reference to the Mississippi Valley," *Mississippi Valley Historical Review*, IX, 185-202.

the Irish added spirit and religious fervor and the German a devotion to the parish organization and to the parochial school. Seldom were the Catholics the wealthy persons of the community and only the few English or Yankee Catholics were welcomed socially by their non-Catholic neighbors. Only in the completely German communities and in the compact Irish settlements of the eastern cities was the English element lacking, with a resultant cultural isolation that delayed the Americanization of the group.

In the nativist Catholic group there has always been an important small, but vigorous, number of converts and their children. It is not known exactly how many converts there were to the Catholic Church among the native Americans during the first two quarters of the century, but some estimates are quite high.[42] These converts were frequently of a higher social position and were less inclined to apologize for their religious differences with the majority. They became far more active than the native Catholics in the propagation and defense of their religion. Notable, besides Eccleston, in the hierarchy were converts Bishop Josue M. Young of Erie and Bishop James F. Wood of Philadelphia; other notable clerical and lay converts were active in the religious discussions of the day. Perhaps none of these outshone in their zeal Isaac Thomas Hecker and Orestes A. Brownson, both of whom became notable for their efforts to show that Catholicism and Americanism were not only compatible but complementary.

In Brownson, particularly, the nativistic attacks on the Irish produced two distinct reactions. Examining the reli-

---

[42] Cf. "Bishop Bruté's Report to Rome in 1836," ed. Thomas T. McAvoy in *Catholic Historical Review*, XXIX (July, 1943), 177-233. Bruté estimated the number of converts very highly. His successor, Bishop Celestine de la Hailandière, was of the same opinion. The chief defect of G. M. Shaugnessy's *Has the Immigrant Kept the Faith?* (New York: The Macmillan Company, 1925) is his failure to estimate properly the number of these converts.

ious attacks on the immigrant, Brownson charged that
uch attacks were un-American. But to the cultural attack
pon the Irish immigrant Brownson was in a certain sense
ympathetic, not, as he vehemently insisted, because he was
nti-Irish but because he felt that the Irish could best pros-
er if they joined themselves to the American cultural ma-
ority in culture and public practice. Brownson saw only
prosperity and advancement for the Irish if they would com-
ine their religious zeal and the advantages of American
ivilization. But to the Irish American press and to Archbishop John Hughes, for whom Catholicism in the English-
peaking world and Irish origins had become almost syn-
onymous, writings of this nature from the pen of Brownson
amounted to a betrayal of the faith. The Catholic press at-
acked Brownson and Archbishop Kenrick allowed his let-
er of approval of *Brownson's Review* to be withdrawn.
Archbishop Hughes publicly rebuked Brownson at a com-
mencement at Fordham in 1856.[43] Disclaiming publicly any
ntention to injure Brownson, Hughes nevertheless wrote
privately to Brownson, ordering him to cease his efforts to
make Americanism and Catholicism compatible. Brownson
fought vainly against the tide and eventually, after making
other tactical errors, had to suspend publication of his
Review in 1864. Likewise, the concern of the American people about the issue of slavery and the approaching Civil
War caused a slackening of interest in the nativistic movement until some years after the war.

Irish immigration never again reached the peak it had attained in the fifties. The Irish who had moved away from
the ports of entry and the industrial concentrations tended
to assimilate themselves into the more native groups in
which they lived, although the compact communities in the

[43] Henry F. Brownson, *Orestes A. Brownson's Latter Life from 1856 to 1876* (Detroit: H. F. Brownson, 1900), pp. 66-75.

eastern cities were more resistant to American culture. Th
Germans, who generally had sufficient means to buy farm
lands, tended to settle in rural communities in the Middl
West.[44] As their numbers increased some also settled in Cir
cinnati, Milwaukee, Chicago, and St. Louis. Only later, a
their cultural isolation began to break down, did they fee
the effects of this cultural amalgamation and offer resistanc
to the Americanizing process, particularly in the so-calle
Cahensly movement.[45]

During the Civil War the Catholics followed the com
munities in which they lived to fight for the North or the
South. The War lifted the nativistic pressure against the
immigrant for a while. Outside of the German communitie
the leadership was divided between the Irish and their de
scendants and the old Maryland-Kentucky group, with the
latter supplying most of the cultural leaven. Public change
symbolized this fact. During the Civil War Archbishop
Hughes was succeeded by the American-born John Mc
Closkey, the first American cardinal, and Archbishop Franci
Kenrick was succeeded by the Kentucky-born Martin John
Spalding. At the close of the conflict the two groups of
native-born and second generation Irish immigrants, to
gether with the other groups not living in compact immi
grant groups, had united to form a distinctive American
Catholic cultural group. With renewed Irish immigration
after the War, American Catholics remained dominantly
Irish in numbers and in public policy but the Catholic cul-

[44] Sister Mary Carol Schroeder, O.S.F., *The Catholic Church in the
Diocese of Vincennes, 1847-1877* (Washington: Catholic University of
America Press, 1946), pp. 70-114, studies this immigration in Indiana; also
Emmet H. Rothan, O.F.M., treats the German Catholic immigration in *The
German Catholic Immigration in the United States (1830-1860)* (Washing-
ton: Catholic University of America Press, 1946), especially chap. 8, "Ger-
man Catholics and Rural Communities."

[45] [The movement's name is derived from the name of its leader, Peter
Cahensly, who proposed that the parish system of the Roman Catholic
Church be organized along ethnic lines, thereby perpetuating national bar-
riers and retarding the orientation of the Roman Catholic immigrants into
the American scene.—Ed.]

re of the whole group became increasingly American.
ter conflicts were to arise; first, between the dominantly
ish hierarchy and the foreign language groups, and then
tween these Americanized groups on the one side and the
ish of the cities and the foreign language groups of the
orthwest on the other. But throughout these later decades
e Americanized Catholic culture remained basically the
me as that of 1860 with later immigrants balanced in
umber by new generations of American-born.

There were other characteristics developed in the forma-
on of this American Catholic culture. The common ele-
ent, of course, has been the fidelity of the whole Catholic
roup to hierarchical rule and to sacramental practices. The
ernness of the American Protestant majority in rejecting
atholics for public office and the continuous propaganda
gainst the church, however, have added to their religious
olidarity. The labors of French, German, and Irish reli-
ious organizations to give Catholic education to the im-
overished immigrant have magnificently supplemented the
fforts of the native-American Catholic to remove any social
tigma from the Catholic group. Only the serious financial
urden of maintaining Catholic churches, separate schools,
nd hospitals out of the lesser material resources has prevented greater progress in raising the level of this American
Catholic culture.

To isolate the contributions of the native-born or the immigrant in the formation of this American Catholic culture
s difficult because the common faith of both groups led
necessarily to a great uniformity in life and practice. The
immigrant did lower the cultural level of the group. The
earlier Catholic group was also outside the majority religious groups of the country, but where some of these native-
born Catholics had before 1830 achieved some social and
political position in dominantly non-Catholic communities,

27

the later immigrants and Catholics generally have achieve such positions only within their own immigrant localit Nor did this condition change quickly. Birth in the Unite States was not sufficient alone to raise the new generatio socially above its parents. As a matter of fact the childre of immigrants who remained in the immigrant milieu d not always attain the cultural level of their parents. Fr quently, also, social distinctions brought from the o country disappeared in the general low level of a mass c immigrants.

Where the immigrant had the means to seek his fortun in the richer opportunities of the West, he usually de veloped the characteristics of the American pioneer, just a the early English Catholic frontiersmen had done in Ke tucky, Indiana, and Ohio. Likewise, where the immigran settled in communities possessing Catholic educational in stitutions, such as the colleges at Bardstown, Georgetowr and Emmitsburg, he usually competed more successfull with the Americans of earlier immigration. But where th immigrant's poverty kept him among crowds of other im poverished immigrants and deprived him of all improve ments except that achieved by mere numbers, as in politics the immigrant was slow to improve or to become Ameri canized in the fullest sense.

Subsequent attempts by the descendants of these Iris immigrants to Americanize later immigrants met with re sistance. By 1860 there was in the Catholic minority a grow ing number of immigrants who spoke a language other thar English. They were at first chiefly from Germany but late included some immigrants from South and Central Europe. Their amalgamation with the English-speaking Catholic group was consequently slower and at times they rebelled against the efforts of the dominantly Irish Catholics to assimilate them. They, perhaps better than the Irish themselves,

w the difference between American culture and the culture
the Irish immigrant. They, too, objected to Americaniza-
n and offered to the English and Irish Catholics of
merican birth and culture much the same resistance as had
en offered by the Irish in 1850.

There were some definite advantages and disadvantages
this composite American Catholic culture that was created
fore 1860. If the Anglo-American group, led by Maréchal,
hitfield, and Eccleston and later by Spalding, Bayley, and
der signalized by activities of such converts as Hecker and
rownson, had retained the dominance over the Catholic
inority, perhaps Catholic colleges and an American Cath-
ic literature in English might have flourished more readily.
stead, the energies of this smaller American group that
ight have developed into higher cultural forms were ab-
orbed in educating and absorbing a larger group which
as without means and, in great numbers, had been derived of education for generations. Likewise, Catholics in
olitics might have advanced more quickly in public office
 they could have escaped the stigma of foreign culture
hich the confusion of religion and politics of the nativistic
eriod ascribed to all Catholics. On the credit side, the ag-
ressive American Catholicism which manifests itself in
ublic demonstrations, the frequentation of the sacraments,
nd the insistence on Catholic parochial schools can be at-
ributed to the tradition of the non-English immigrants,
rish, German, Polish, and the like, who came from Catholic
egions of Europe and who saw more quickly the dangers
o religious faith in the non-religious public schools and the
dvantages of a Catholic milieu.

Both natives and immigrants benefited from the freedom
f frontier America but the native who was able to remain
way from the industrialized urban conditions acquired
more quickly a distinctly American spirit. The fact that

Catholics who congregated in compact Irish and Germ
settlements in the mill towns, in the larger cities, or even
the immigrant colonization projects of the west made slow
progress in accepting American cultural ideals can be e
plained chiefly by the absence in their communities of me:
bers of the Anglo-American Catholic group which h
formed the leaven of the Maryland and Kentucky commu:
ties. Brownson's analysis of this fact was received angrily
the eighteen-fifties. But even then there were some wl
sensed the formation of a distinctly American Catho.
culture. The writer "M" in the January, 1857, *Metropolita*
the chief Catholic magazine of the time, commenting cr
ically on Brownson's essays on nativism, sized up the situ
tion quite well despite his sympathy for the immigra:
group. "The native Catholics of Maryland and Kentuc!
furnish their full quota of priests and religious, and b
fore there is an increase in the number of native pries
there must be an increase in the number of native Catholic
As a general thing Irish priests, *ceteris paribus*, are the be
for Irish people and it will be found most likely that tl
relative number of native priests and native Catholics wi
under God's providence, augment in proper ratio."[46]

Like so many of the Irish Catholics of the period, "M
did not fully understand that Brownson and Bishops Timo:
McGill, and Whelan had no doubt about the faith or pa
triotism of the immigrant Catholic. But these native Amer
cans did recognize that there was a distinction betwee
American culture and that of the immigrant. They wer
convinced that the immigrant could profit by the social an
cultural spirit of Americans. The attitude of the Irish im

[46] *The Metropolitan* (Baltimore), January, 1857, pp. 720-23. This ed
torial is a comment on the article of Archbishop Hughes on the Cathol:
press in the December, 1856, issue (pp. 629-61) and on Brownson's crit
cism of the Archbishop's statement in the January, 1857, issue of *Browr
son's Quarterly Review*, XIV, 114-41.

migrant of the eighteen-fifties was best personified by Archbishop John Hughes. Archbishop Hughes never seemed to understand fully that there had always been American Catholics or that there was no conflict between being an Anglo-American and being a Catholic.[47] Faced with American nativists who were hostile to their religion, the Catholic immigrants can be excused for not realizing that to prefer the ideals of the Anglo-American Catholics was perhaps a greater loyalty to Catholicism and certainly a better service to American Catholic culture. Repelled by the nativists, the immigrants who numerically dominated the Catholic group held back from the common culture and suffered some of the cultural evils which Brownson had predicted as a result of this partial isolation. For the eighty years since 1860 American Catholic culture has risen just as quickly as the immigrant group has been able to Americanize its cultural tradition. Similarly the non-Catholic religious people have shown a better understanding of Catholic culture just in proportion as they have been able to see that the foreign elements of the Catholic culture are the accidents of history and not part of their universal faith. Those who reject that faith have other reasons for rejecting American Catholic culture. But the gradual Americanization of the masses of non-English Catholic immigrants, with the old Anglo-American Catholic group as a nucleus, is an understandable process and one as American as all the other combinations of immigration and the frontier which constitute our American civilization.

[47] In his "Lecture on the Present Condition and Prospects of the Catholic Church in the United States" he does recognize the existence of the early Maryland Catholics but when he speaks of Catholics in the American Revolution he mentions only Irish names.

For Further Reading

STER MARY AUGUSTINA RAY, B.V.M. *American Opinion of Roman Catholicism in the Eighteenth Century*. New York: Columbia University Press, 1936.

DAMS, WILLIAM F. *Ireland and Irish Immigration to the New World from 1815 to the Famine*. New Haven: Yale University Press, 1932.

ILLINGTON, RAY A. *The Protestant Crusade (1800-1860)*. New York: The Macmillan Company, 1938.

TEPHENSON, GEORGE M. "Nativism in the Forties and Fifties, with Special Reference to the Mississippi Valley," *Mississippi Valley Historical Review*, IX (1922), 185-202.

HAUGNESSY, GERALD M. *Has the Immigrant Kept the Faith?* New York: The Macmillan Company, 1925.

OTHAN, EMMET H. *The German Catholic Immigration in the United States*. Washington: Catholic University of America Press, 1946.

ELIKAN, JAROSLAV. *The Riddle of Roman Catholicism*. New York and Nashville: Abingdon Press, 1959.

Facet Books Already Published

storical Series:

1. *Were Ancient Heresies Disguised Social Movements?*
   by A. H. M. Jones. 1966
2. *Popular Christianity and the Early Theologians*
   by H. J. Carpenter. 1966
3. *Tithing in the Early Church*
   by Lukas Vischer (translated by Robert C. Schultz). 1966
4. *Jerusalem and Rome*
   by Hans von Campenhausen and Henry Chadwick. 1966
5. *The Protestant Quest for a Christian America 1830-1930*
   by Robert T. Handy. 1967
6. *The Formation of the American Catholic Minority 1820-1860*
   by Thomas T. McAvoy. 1967
7. *A Critical Period in American Religion 1875-1900*
   by Arthur M. Schlesinger, Sr. 1967
8. *Images of Religion in America*
   by Jerald C. Brauer. 1967

blical Series:

1. *The Significance of the Bible for the Church*
   by Anders Nygren (translated by Carl Rasmussen). 1963
2. *The Sermon on the Mount*
   by Joachim Jeremias (translated by Norman Perrin). 1963
3. *The Old Testament in the New*
   by C. H. Dodd. 1963
4. *The Literary Impact of the Authorized Version*
   by C. S. Lewis. 1963
5. *The Meaning of Hope*
   by C. F. D. Moule. 1963
6. *Biblical Problems and Biblical Preaching*
   by C. K. Barrett. 1964

7. *The Genesis Accounts of Creation*
   by Claus Westermann (translated by Norman E. Wagne
   1964

8. *The Lord's Prayer*
   by Joachim Jeremias (translated by John Reumann). 19

9. *Only to the House of Israel? Jesus and the Non-Jews*
   by T. W. Manson. 1964

10. *Jesus and the Wilderness Community at Qumran*
    by Ethelbert Stauffer (translated by Hans Spalteho
    1964

11. *Corporate Personality in Ancient Israel*
    by H. Wheeler Robinson. 1964

12. *The Sacrifice of Christ*
    by C. F. D. Moule. 1964

13. *The Problem of the Historical Jesus*
    by Joachim Jeremias (translated by Norman Perrin).
    1964

14. *A Primer of Old Testament Text Criticism*
    by D. R. Ap-Thomas. 1966

15. *The Bible and the Role of Women*
    by Krister Stendahl (translated by Emilie Sander). 19

16. *Introduction to Pharisaism*
    by W. D. Davies. 1967

17. *Man and Nature in the New Testament*
    by C. F. D. Moule. 1967

18. *The Lord's Supper According to the New Testament*
    by Eduard Schweizer (translated by James M. Davis
    1967

19. *The Psalms: A Form-Critical Introduction*
    by Herman Gunkel (translated by Thomas Horner). 196

Social Ethics Series:

1. *Our Calling*
   by Einar Billing (translated by Conrad Bergendoff). 196

2. *The World Situation*
   by Paul Tillich. 1965

3. *Politics as a Vocation*
   by Max Weber (translated by H. H. Gerth and C. Wrigh
   Mills). 1965

4. *Christianity in a Divided Europe*
   by Hanns Lilje. 1965

5. *The Bible and Social Ethics*
   by Hendrik Kraemer. 1965

6. *Christ and the New Humanity*
   by C. H. Dodd. 1965

7. *What Christians Stand For in the Secular World*
   by William Temple. 1965

8. *Legal Responsibility and Moral Responsibility*
   by Walter Moberly. 1965

9. *The Divine Command: A New Perspective on Law and Gospel*
   by Paul Althaus (translated by Franklin Sherman). 1966

10. *The Road to Peace*
    by John C. Bennett, Kenneth Johnstone, C. F. von Weizsächer, Michael Wright. 1966

11. *The Idea of a Natural Order: With an Essay on Modern Asceticism*
    by V. A. Demant. 1966

12. *Kerygma, Eschatology, and Social Ethics*
    by Amos N. Wilder. 1966

13. *Affluence and the Christian*
    by Hendrik van Oyen (translated by Frank Clarke). 1966

14. *Luther's Doctrine of the Two Kingdoms*
    by Heinrich Bornkamm (translated by Karl H. Hertz). 1966

15. *Christian Decision in a Nuclear Age*
    by T. R. Milford. 1967

16. *Law and Gospel*
    by Werner Elert (translated by Edward H. Schroeder). 1967

Body, 12 on 13 Garamond
Display, Garamond
Paper, White Spring Grove, E. F.